Under the
Tented Skin

C. KUBASTA

UNSOLICITED
PRESS
PORTLAND, OREGON
EST 2012

Through a Project Grant for Artists, the writing of this book was supported in part by the Nevada Arts Council and the National Endowment for the Arts.

For information contact:

Unsolicited Press

Portland, Oregon

www.unsolicitedpress.com

orders@unsolicitedpress.com

619-354-8005

Cover Design: Kathryn Gerhardt

Editor: Summer Stewart

ISBN: 978-1-963115-79-6

Poems

for Bren

Under the Tented Skin

C. KUBASTA

250 word bio, *preferably* third-person

Offering can mean a thing presented or sacrificed "in worship or devotion," "in tribute or as token of esteem." My father gave me *The Shorter Oxford English Dictionary* because he didn't know about rows of fabric-clad volumes full of citations. That's what I wanted. All the possibilities of that verbal noun.

That's what you think when you receive a Facebook message from a former teacher. When a person is chosen, complex feelings may accompany being chosen.

What it means to be a very smart girl, a girl who can go far—beyond where you are: which is why he takes such interest. Why he worries, years later, because he didn't _____ you, that you might think yourself "unattractive" or "unworthy" or *unlovable*.

You're told you've always been precocious. That at your first doctor's appointment, you flirted with the doctor when he changed your diaper.

Each story presents a mirror of itself:

You dream about a species of hummingbird that flies very low to the ground; dies if looked at too long. You spend your days pointing it out, then begging people to look away.

When asked why you're a poet, you answer instead why you're a good eater:

there's nothing I won't try / I don't throw the skins away / and I've been known to gnaw a bone.

(Mis)Appropriations

Covetousness

Owls are all kinds of omens: if an owl
flies in the daylight someone
nearby will come to harm. Owl-song
between houses sings of a girl-become-woman,
that archaic threshold crossed.
Some traditions hold owls the souls of women,
either sacred or witches.

We have messaged each other twice
in twenty years—but today I'm thinking
about the time an owl landed in the passenger
seat of your car and you drove on, frozen
unsure what to do. You looking at the owl
& the owl looking at you.

Athena's mascot was the owl, sitting
on her shoulder, assisting with her blind side. In college
my mother sent me a small glass owl, hoping. Home
one break, she warned me my diaphragm
might need retreading. My youngest nephew
likes to play which god or goddess we'd each be—
first he gave me Medusa,

and I told him there was nothing
wrong with turning a man to stone.

I lied; the year after we finally ended, we
still talked quite a bit, about
if it was really over—and other things
I don't think I should say. The owl
in your car a perfect object lesson. If an owl
is nailed to the door of a house
evil stays away. This Christmas I've been
following updates of a college friend losing
her husband—diagnosis to death
in less than a month. Hammer that feathered carcass
to the barn door and keep each sheep
warm & dry, away from wolves.

I will always be hungry
for news of you: harbinger
of owl calls, seer who could never
make out the shape of wings
silhouetted against the sun.
Even if we knew to cook owl eyes
to ash and eat them by the handful, we
ignore what's right in front of us.

Your name makes me flinch; your wife's too. Even
after my kin relented and gave me Aphrodite,

I knew I was only every character
in every story in every tradition who died
from looking back. You drove with me
in the passenger seat for years
and we pretended we weren't afraid.

Things I Would Tell a Daughter: A Poetics

If you sit outside in the dark, things sound larger & closer than they are.

To navigate a crowd, lower your shoulders but keep your elbows out.

It is better to be interesting than pretty.

You will either be sexualized, or a mother; beyond this is a space unchartered.

It is always about power but it should never be about power.

Stay attuned to groups of women, their intimate meteorologies.

Success arrives in the guise of your first stalker.

On old maps, cartographers wrote/may have written "Here there be monsters." Or drawn images of monstrous things, their imaginations limited to versions of the known world.

we imagine this a common practice : we myth-make this fiction into fact

(Most of these maps were just Drawing-Room Pretties for hanging on walls—never meant for navigation.)

Stay attuned to groups of women: the Drawing-Room Pretties, the Monstrous-Who-Are-Versions-of-the-Known-World. Look for the door beyond the door beyond the door.

Sound so large & close no one will sit out in the dark.

Poem About How J Always Calls It

After several days of no-fish fishing
there's finally a single walleye on the stringer
and we can't decide what to do about dinner
so he hangs it off the side of the pier
until later. She looks up—

that's like locking a girl in the basement

—as the day wears he checks it, and
even after we've moved on to another menu
he leaves it for a while, says he's "teaching
it a lesson."

Unkindness

Of all possible you's, I'm most invested in *Schrodinger's You*—
you and not you simultaneously, always and never.

One way to tell *the* story is to write
about when childhood ends—
what this means depends on positionality, point of view.
Address those who were to care for you, cocoon you

and either did or didn't, who tried
and failed, or were complicit
in that undoing: which [you] would [you] write to?

You once told me every poet has a poem about a crow
but lately I've been thinking maybe it's a raven—at a distance

it can be hard to tell the difference:
listen for a lower, throatier call,
and look at tail shape. I've been watching still living

things carried away in talons, twitching.
I thought crows only scavenged, but both species
predate eggs & nestlings, and ravens sometimes

take on larger things: rodents & other small mammals
—or mass together
to kill newborn livestock if they're not moving much.

It could be either post-mortem scavenging
of a stillborn or opportunistic predation, but a flock of ravens
during calving season makes ranchers nervous. Two or more

ravens is called an Unkindness. If you've heard
the Eastern Cottontail meeting death
you know it sounds like a child—when darkness
smothers all sound, you sit upright in bed
thinking, "What now?"
wondering if it's something you have to see to,
or if it can wait until morning. You wait 'til morning.

Comstockery

The only waters you won't drown in
are the caul's. Sailors will pay
for a bit of it, if
you're savvy enough
to save the membrane.
Midwives press paper
to the infant's face
and gently pull away, preserving
the amniotic sac
and minimizing scars.

The only morsel you can't devour
is yourself, but folklore
about too much desire
offers this tell:
watch for half-eaten lips.
Never sated, you'll see
them bitten and swollen, licked
and chapped, too many teeth
in a red-rimmed mouth—
by then you're caught.

Sharp eyes screen the mail
for mentions
of acts and anatomy,
devices and predilections,
catching everything
from medical knowledge
to philosophy to women whispering
in a well-honed language
of euphemism. Each instance
punishable by five years hard labor.

Immorality knows only itself;
the same with purity. Both
circle an ungovernable
center named *lust*.
Comstock wrote it "sears
the conscience." Rising
waters, swallowed mouthfuls, stories
made to explain this face or that,
each beloved by someone, even
yours in the morning, reflected back.

Trying Hard

Drunks die from drink and at their funerals friends show up midway through the service, unsteady in inappropriate shoes. Or with a fresh shave from a shaky hand, wearing their one pair of good pants that still aren't funeral pants. Someone shushes someone else—the shushing louder than whatever came before but they've never been good at moderating their behavior, their volume or tone, and grief undoes them completely. People of big gestures: big hurt and big love.

Like the woman who takes a chair in the family row: eyeliner top and bottom, inner and outer rims, and doesn't understand why the seat was empty to begin with. *She is family* she explains to the uptight bitch who tries to make her move. *This was her favorite* she hisses as she adds a bottle to the funeral home's careful array of arrangements and plants. At the luncheon following, the drunk's friends drink their lunches at the bar and keep passing on the sandwiches.

At a good drunk's funeral, even though it's family only, more than family show up. When a good drunk drinks to bury whatever they need to bury, it stays buried—at least when they're drunk—and all that comes out is love. Everywhere they go they collect people who need them:

"You're my family," they say. "I love you," to everyone. Anyone who needs to hear it—so many of us need to hear it—believe it, remembering that time we met the good drunk.

At a bad drunk's funeral, there's no need to restrict entry. Empty chair empty chair empty chair. Alert to Rorschach-laughter, the slim edge when it all begins to turn. The obituary spare of stories, all subtext.

If you're parsing the difference between good drunks and bad drunks, you're a bad drunk. Or you love one. Or you're trying hard not to—

Gas & Smokes

At the non-chain, Mom & Pop station, where the lake's curve
fattens, I stop for gas & smokes, a six-pack or liquor
outside the municipal limits. Either the woman or the man
works the late shift, and sometimes
they work together. I don't know what
they are to each other, but about
the same age—late fifties or early sixties. A bell above

the door, point-of-sale displays, hand-lettered signs. Bait
swim in a trio of sinks with circulating water, by the freezers
with pizzas and gallon ice cream growing rimes

of frost. And on
ce, ringing up my smokes, he said, "Put out your hand," and w
hen I did, he put a candy bar in it
from the daily-special display. (I don't remember what kind,
but the wrapper said *King Size*—the wra
pper said *12 Inches*). The man said
"Do you like that? Do you lik
e how that feels in your hand?" I looked
for a security came
ra, estimated the distance
to the door, no oth

er cars in the lot, under the pumps.
"I don't care for sweets," I an
swered and put it back, took
my smokes, left.

Two days later I was back for gas and they were both
there and the woman took care of me and the man
made no eye contact. I didn't say anything.

Tonight, the woman counts wax worms
into little plastic cups lined with sawdust,
some stacked into an intricate pyramid
for the point-of-sale, $1.00 each.

"Maggots," she says, as she sets down her work; trucks
pulling trailers under the glared light
of the pumps. "For the Fisheree?" She nods & rings
me up. "They turn my stomach." And I almost tell her.

Hindsight

I.

My father writes about his tubes: the one
from the kidney to the bladder, the one
that makes its way out. He is learning
email, the trickiness of tone, how to craft
subject lines. Vast improvement since the unfortunate

"I have cancer" missive, delivered with a shrug. This one
tagged "Today I learned a lot about kidney stones,"
the message full of details: a log of times and pain levels
a description of the little screen
used to catch it, the crystalline edges
to be analyzed. At the ER, during the scan
they are able to watch its movement
but have lost the larger one that measured

nine millimeters, the one they were unable
to zap & pulverize; it's gone, disappeared
as if it never was.

II.

To kill two birds, a professor of biology & biblical literature
points out how human males lack a baculum, how scripture
lies: the story of Adam's rib taken to create Eve. He writes

the Hebrew *tzela* can mean rib, or support beam. We can lay
our bodies down, male & female, count the bony spines
under skin, two by two. The professor suggests the reference

was a "circumlocution"—perhaps we Eves
made of supporting structures
osseous matter disappeared, as if it never was.

III.

When interviewing a victim, be aware that inconsistencies
may be an effect of trauma. Victims may be unable
to give a log of times
and pain levels. They may speak in outbursts
conflicting statements, non sequiturs, circumlocutions.
Or they may not speak

at all, not then. Perhaps you once called something out
when touched, something you don't—can't—remember.
Something you won't repeat here.

The Myth of the Underage Woman

What I think is a hummingbird,
heart rate more than a thousand beats a minute, resting
respiration in the hundreds—is a sphinx moth: still beautiful,
somewhat rare, nectar feeder, honey stealer. It courts
confusion. This isn't about birds at all.

What looked sodden & substantial under the surface
is just water contacting water, aping solid.

Even a dream where your sister offers
a bushel of bird beaks means nothing finally.

Female dragonflies of the *A. Juncea* species
fall from the sky to avoid copulating with males.
Cellophane wings glitter the ground; underbellies of
thorax showing. The observant scientists note:
This is an atypical posture for a dragonfly.
The underbelly of the thorax is called the sternum;
the females assume this posture to mimic death.
When threatened, the human

response includes an instant increase
in heart rate & blood pressure.

Muscles, lungs, brain bathed in blood—the flow swells
hundreds of percent to arm us for whatever is coming.

It must mean something: the way you turn toward it, or
cower & cover, hands splayed over sternum, wings still.

I Am Not Talking about Bees

The bee box arrives, its furious Latin or Greek:
menarche & all that. But
you know what this is for, this is not for
you. Nubility comes later, maybe. You are neither
predictable nor consistent
in your intervals, your duration, your pain.

Less celebrated, the hive depends
on non-fertile female worker bees. We clean & build,
forage & gather, guard. We
are often short-lived, our bodies
collect at the mouth of hives, we sacrificial females
we noble honey-drudges. Few songs sung
for this thousand-strong caste.

For the woman who doesn't mother, others caution:
you will regret your choice.
For the woman who mothers, no one
asks: do you regret your choice?
But some do—there is research on regretting motherhood,
but it is the great taboo. The behavioral ecologist said,
"The ability to birth fertilized eggs—
to mate—is called a 'privilege.'"

(That's just how she put it).
The way we word platitudes: *Children are a joy;*
Children are a blessing, encode non-choice
into our Cultural DNA.

Since stopping my fallopian tubes with nickel
and overgrowth flesh, I've become
predictable & consistent in intervals, duration, pain.
I exceed my own estimation
of absorptive materials, the ticking of the clock.
I throw clots, accumulated endometrium.
(Brood cells uncleaned). The women I know
are long past this—menopausal, or hysterectomied.
The aged queens ask why
I save this equipment, this empty room
this deflated balloon.

As if it only values with use, as if
it doesn't reside inside me, isn't me.

As if I haven't stored things there: an armoire; two tube TV's—
their elegant curved backs, outdated, but still working; some
clothes I may fit into again.

The nuptial flight marks the position of the hive, days
after the Queen emerges from her cell;
other flights last only minutes, long enough to collect

what she needs of drones before returning
to keep the factory humming. Sometimes
she cannot or will not fly; sometimes she leaves.
A hive without a proper queen is doomed.

My Students Talk about Snakes

how the large ones are less frightening than the small ones
how they are always docile until they aren't

one woman talks about feeding, how mice
aren't cheap—she used to get them free
from a nearby school with a research lab
once they were done with them. some
had strange bodies or obvious
things wrong. some looked whole but her snake
would approach and move away, tuned
to some interior wrong

one doodles pictures in their notes & when I hand them back
I've added a snake. in the garden, trees & green
some birds, but there's always a snake.
in one of my recurring nightmares, what looks

green, the roped vines or hanging bits of some wilding plant
soon-to-bloom reveal themselves to be snakes
looped around branches, patterned
like light & shadow. some say
the large ones are more docile,

until they aren't. you dream you shoot
your dog. in the dream, you try to hide
the evidence—you try to get the dog alone
to finish it off. you ask

what this means and I say it: the dog is you.
we dream over and over the thing we cannot kill.

I've become attuned to men & their cant:
the angle of their bodies, their hypocrisies. in my dreams

of tree-roped snakes, I freeze, caught—I must live
with them now, hoping
they sense my interior wrong, a tongue-flick of scent
that marks me unwise prey.

The Burying

I should call home more often but you only tell me is who is dying or dead. This game of cat & mouse memory, some childhood you imagine I had: "You know ___, they were a ___, married so-and-so?" I don't, but try to remember names from one call to another to comfort you if that's needed: what it means when your bartender's wife dies, or you end up forced into some favor you've refused.

On the borders of two modern-day countries, archeologists found a nearly-six-foot-tall skeleton with a striking ornament. She's estimated to be 28-34 years old, but articles call her *girl*. They call her ornament a *prosthetic* or *artificial* eye; larger than the socket and painted gold. She would have worn it on thin strings, opaque shining, a soothsayer or truthteller. Uncovered in the dirt, a purpled orb—clouded with age and we cannot look away.

At the backyard of childhood's remembering, I see three dog bodies. No one claimed them. They'd starved, I was told, because they were someone's else's responsibility; and that was repeated, telephone-style, until the spring came and the carcasses needed tending. In the saying of names today, that someone's name is among the dead and all I can think of is those dogs.

When I say no to something now—grown—I've been told I'm good at it. At boundaries. Naming things unsaid. I've mostly run across depictions of prosthetic eyes in books symbolizing vulnerability: beside Hulga's undoing in the hayloft, or back-and-forth in Kevin's hands as some awful talisman. Adaptive equipment made abjectification. Here's the thing: he must have heard the dogs—barking & then no barking, slowly or all at once.

In an antique mall in Indiana I found a salesman sample case of glass eyes, and they were shaped differently than I expected—slightly oblong, a divot in the middle. The Persian woman's eye was a half sphere, hollow & light, worn close to the empty socket. But she was a girl once, and who knows what she knew, what she took to her grave.

Obituary for a Monster

Hate feeds a girl, but it can't be the only thing
she eats. To understand, we need to expand
our definition of so many ideas—weigh immediate
aftermath against the following days, the next few months,
even the years that will make up what she calls her life.
Without flexibility, a jury may remain

forever deadlocked. Punching holes of darker night
in the sky, bats fly out. Their name
means "hand-wing" in Greek; at the tips of their span

are flexible bones we might call "fingers."

In colonies, they hang upside down, huddled
side-by-side to expend as little energy as possible.
Flight an enormous cost—the super-heated body
with its paper doll skin carries, but is not consumed by,
things that kill us. At the end of their day,
beginning of ours, upside-down bones
webbed in the brown-grey, they fall prey
instead to White Nose Syndrome—spread cave
by cave, sleep by sleep.

From the area roped off for visitors
and media, cameras flash. Disinfect clothes
to prevent spread. We've moved
further and further into their territory.

When we lived in that cut-up house's lower, joists
precarious on the crumbling basement's dirt walls,
my job was the mice and you handled the bats.
I remember you in your boxer shorts, broom swinging wildly,
as the cat leapt four feet high for the careering visitor.
You connected and it crossed the room
to slap wetly against my face.

I woke up with this poem's opening line in my head
the day after Weinstein was found guilty of two of five counts.
Each day, he arrived at the courthouse shambling,
stooped over a walker. Picture after picture after
picture of the now-old man looking harmless. See also:

the way a community of bats both protects and endangers;
the way their wing bones are both light and dense;
although delicate, tears in the wing repair quickly.

Bat echolocation is subtle enough to catch small insects
in near or total dark, but I've always been afraid, imagining
my hair a trap, and their tonal clicks a panic tantrum.
A bat caught out in the daylight looks so vulnerable, apart

from its others, webbed-wing skin translucent, and milk teeth
hidden, but the one time I tried to kill one, I couldn't.

After that bat hit my face, I couldn't shower long enough.

We revert to platitudes to distance ourselves
from the terrible thing. We know
what we are saying is insufficient & inadequate
but we cannot say anything else. What we mean is:
I'm so glad it wasn't me. I'm so so glad it wasn't me.

House Wren

A bird in the house
means we may lose
our best cow
in the coming year.
But there's no husbandry
here—animal or other.

A bird in the house
may predict death,
but this one is neither
white nor black—instead
a dirty brownish-grey, feathers
disheveled. Bad fledge. Maybe
mite-infested, it careers
room to room
after slipping in over
the storm door's edge.

We try to trick it to safety.
Small moves, calm voices—you
even whistle at one point, pretending
to be other than you are. Perhaps

the house seemed inviting:
soft glow at the windows,
a few degrees warmer
than night. But some
cannot live like this, no matter
how soft the bed, how
well-chosen the hues.
We make promises
to negotiate the future, but

it's the present that doesn't work.

Within six years, selecting
for *tameness*—or calm—
resulted in quick changes
in a population of silver foxes,
and much of what we know
about domestication
comes from this study:

they licked hands,
wagged tails, could be
picked up & petted.

One summer I worked a farm and
they started with pigs,
but the piglets kept escaping

the pen to find us
in the fields, weeding
between rows. They'd play-bow
and wag their tails. One of the farmers
reminded me part of my payment
in fall would be bacon. I'd lead
future-delicious-them
back to the barn. Some structures

are traps and some animals
won't be tamed. Like zebras.
Maybe their environment has too many predators,
and no alliance with man is safety.

That bird isn't going to make it
and neither are we.

January in Wisconsin

The dog paces all night, panting, so I tell you about working third shift at the dementia home — walking people back to their rooms: a dose of comfort with the same conversations no pretense of orienting. With F, we talked about her daughters and picked an outfit for the next day, always the same outfit, and always the same stories, and I never met the daughters. With E, he'd start flirting but become combative and accuse me of stealing things, often parts of himself. I'm not comparing people to my dog, it's just the night restlessness reminded me   likely we all end up wandering, looking for something. I'll end up there: a rented room with paid caregivers, and that's okay. That's what I told my grandmother when   she said that's the reason to have children.

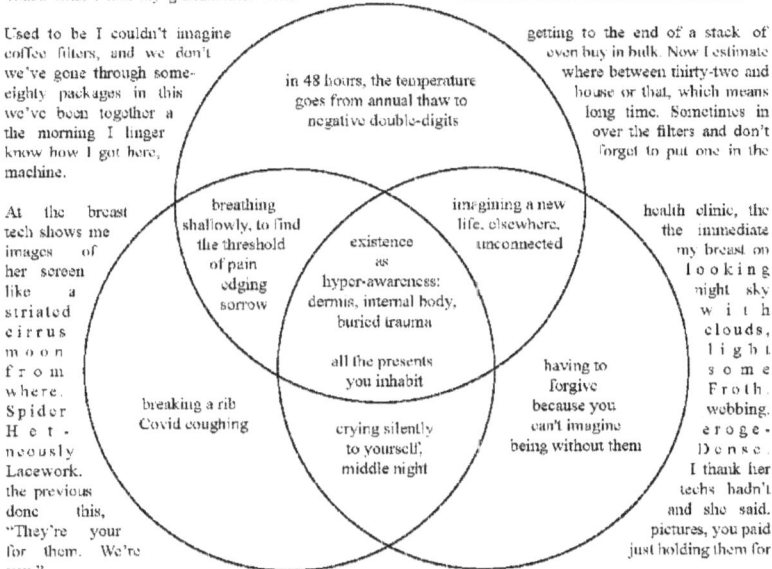

Used to be I couldn't imagine coffee filters, and we don't we've gone through some-eighty packages in this the morning I linger know how I got here, machine.

in 48 hours, the temperature goes from annual thaw to negative double-digits

getting to the end of a stack of even buy in bulk. Now I estimate where between thirty-two and house or that, which means long time. Sometimes in over the filters and don't forget to put one in the

At the breast tech shows me images of her screen like a striated cirrus moon from where. Spider Het-neously Lacework. the previous done this, "They're your for them. We're you."

breathing shallowly, to find the threshold of pain edging sorrow

imagining a new life. elsewhere, unconnected

existence as hyper-awareness: dermis, internal body, buried trauma

all the presents you inhabit

breaking a rib Covid coughing

having to forgive because you can't imagine being without them

crying silently to yourself, middle night

health clinic, the the immediate my breast on looking night sky with clouds, light some Froth. webbing. eroge- Dense. I thank her techs hadn't and she said. pictures, you paid just holding them for

We keep an eye on that one   lymph node.   Enlargement and what looks like calcifications are likely the result of new work. She'd complimented the arm & shoulder piece, asked if she could touch it. I appreciate the ask. I don't know how I got here. The metal oxides in tattoo pigments are radiopaque. Parts of myself I've carefully hidden keep escaping, mimicking disease processes on imaging. Sentinel lymph node. Auxiliary. Potential Understaging. Irritant & nacre. I walk them back to their rooms, go through the routine of putting them to bed. They refuse: opaque, enlarged, juddered edges on radiographic film.

Of Ruins and Follies

The failed subdivision has empty cul-de-sacs
but no people, an asphalt thoroughfare
split with mature plantings and one four-way stop
that everyone barrels through—my favorite
back way through town. Charmless as middle age, as late
capitalism, I love it unreasonably, the way
I cannot give up on my father.

When my parents were married, we had three
coffee table books: *The Best of Rube Goldberg*,
101 Uses for a Dead Cat, and
how to make your own ancient ruins—with diagrams
of chisels and masonry and inserting invasive plants.
Our cat was a tortoiseshell. If a ruin
is *an accidental aesthetic object*
then what I want to talk about are follies:

no purpose other than decorative, and
often hiding something. British gardeners
loved them, made to look like ruins.

I'm thinking of the pretty smart girls in high school
who got married because they got pregnant

whether they wanted to or not
whether they liked the guy or not.

The one whose husband joined up
and she had the baby while he was overseas
and they divorced as soon as he got back
and their daughter is amazing and they're both good parents
but they can barely look at each other.

The one where the marriage got her
out of the house—oldest daughter to so many
younger siblings—and that got her out of the church
and they left town altogether and her family
says they have no daughter.

The one where they hurried up before anyone even knew
and she lost the pregnancy before anyone even knew
but they didn't call it off because people would know
and now they have a few and the youngest just graduated.

Nobody says the word *ruined* anymore
and if we're going to put something pretty in our gardens
it better be useful. When people say something "worked out,"
they're only talking about the ending.
They pretend to forget the beginning,
and skip real fast through the middle.

Desiring, with Embedded Tankas

I had a boyfriend once, who believed in Decomposition. We swerved his truck to each hummock of roadkill, careening back roads, finishing the work of some come-before traveler, flattening carcasses into unrecognizability. *Less for the highway crew*, he'd say. *They're already dead*, he'd say. *Returning them to nature.* Some things just are, "belief" is not the right word, verbed or not. Common egrets / known as the Great White Heron / gather at the maw / of the stream that feeds the lake, / too many to count. I thought /

them solitary birds. I had a boyfriend once, who wouldn't sleep with me. He didn't believe in latex, artificial hormones, the calendar or his own control. *I can't,* he said, *risk bringing a life into this world I'm not prepared to care for.* I'd plead for skin, sheathed in multiple prophylactics, only succeed

occasionally. / At certain times, lake flies clot / the air,
thrumming, their / mouthless bodies. My body / hungers, vibrates
engines with /

no discernible center. I have a friend who careens between dark places; imagines his beloved with secret lives & loves or the girl of his dreams, placid and perfect and untouched. He snares along the creek bed in season, returns to red flags

awave. To harvest / a turtle, you'll need a tub / to trap the blood.
So / much blood, an oil-slick pooling. / But the meat is tender,
caught /

between clades. On the river road to work, two cars ahead the driver clips a squirrel, and the wind catches its body, wiffling the stunned creature aloft, little kite. As I approach it makes for the side of the road, dragging the weight of itself / with front paws extended, taut. / *I should square the tires* / and end the animal pain / but the body wants its wants.

Circumlocutions

Cardinal Directions

Trying to bring contraband home, we pack
the checked luggage, send it
with the grandparents. Some shells, a piece
of brain coral, but it gets pulled
in the screening. I have something small

in my carry-on. I've had luck
with small transgressions, little souvenirs.
Once I brought back a turtle shell
wrapped in dirty panties
and even though it triggered a bad check, the screener
stopped, reluctant to work
his way through. Maybe I've just
been lucky—maybe. Still, I think
the way to hide something precious or prohibited
is to wrap it in something more so.

The woman taking orders for coffee at the gate
had a bleeding mouth
and she kept licking the new red, or wiping
her lip with her sleeve and looking
checking to see if & how it was healing.

Maybe a split lip from some
innocuous event—maybe.

A line from Akhmatova reads, "We have learned that
blood smells only of blood" and maybe—but there's also

taste, and this sends me down a rabbit hole to childhood:

any wound within reach of the early antiseptic of ourselves,
each jagged-toothed cut from a fall on asphalt
stippled the sweet red insides of the mouth
tasting as we run to catch up, brush ourselves off, keep
going, after friends or siblings or cousins or whatever

we were chasing. I remember
a curtain-darkened room midday—his voice
saying "iron filings," my limbs
stretched toward the cardinal directions
of box spring corners. I don't know
if that was in reference to smell or taste
but I recall relief in that moment.
But we were in childhood

a moment ago, and I've ruined it.
Akhmatova wasn't writing about childhood

either, although she began with the smells
of wild honey & a girl's mouth.

Maybe childhood ends when we learn
to hide the precious thing. Maybe
our own blood smells
only of blood. The precious thing

has different names, and some
of them are dirty. Someone might be
afraid to touch it; someone—
maybe—will uncover it. What matters

is the curtain-dark room, and whether one of you will name it:
childhood is over when we know blood other than our own.

Terrible Beauties

I will greatly multiply
your sorrow and your conception; in sorrow
you shall bring forth children; and your desire
shall be to your husband, and he
shall rule over you.

Parse the linking of sorrow & conception, sorrow
& labor. A literal translation of Genesis 3:16 reads
toward your husband your desire—
make what you wish of the absent verb.

Discern all the possible meanings of desire.

Take this complex mess & go.
This violent craving for a thing, it tramples.

Our problem has always been disordered desire.

We have no idea what tree, what fruit, so neither know
what flower. The Talmud offers options: grapevine,
fig, or wheat—each with their own logic. The Midrash
suggests it is not named so the species be saved tarnish.

Maybe the flower was particularly stunning
(like a hammer orchid or a bloom of compressed
inflorescence, single bract)—and the woman,
new to all things, did not know beauty's primary purpose
was reproduction. Each blossom had a woman's house
& a man's house and would fruit. More likely,

it wasn't special to anyone but her. I loved a man once
with no discernible navel, but he was no Adam.

Out with new people, a woman mentions her full breast
tattoo, and I ask if it covers the nipple.
Our mutual friend interjects,
"She doesn't have nipples." Her husband's
head bobs up & down. *Oh*, I say, *oh*.
A magnolia blooms, line work and shading,
dark center slightly off center
where the flower's ovary would be, where
the areola would be. She shows me
on her phone. At my next appointment, I ask the artist
about working the piloerector muscles, eager-to-pucker,
and he says it's a little trickier. Not as difficult as other places
and he names our interiors, our sensitivities, our
almost-always covered, but I get caught
on the inside of the navel.

Some argue even as adults our navels still house
a latent structure tied to bladder or liver. How tender,
that place that tied & fed us before we were us.
I shudder at even the most superficial of needles
denting dense flesh. Some swear by Vitamin E
or commercial blends like BIO-Oil to lessen
the appearance of scars; I mention this because
you might want to wear sleeves everywhere, every day.

You could. In certain jobs, people wear sleeves, every day.
Some people use tattoos to mark an overcoming, to remake
the body after trauma—like mastectomy—thickened flesh
as frame or inception for some new, profane creation;
but I've never seen it with those kind of scars. After the Fall,

He asked: *Who told you that you were naked?*
What is it that you have done? Those of us new to nothing,
understand desire has always been a burden.

The Girl with No Hands

In stories like this, everything seems so simple at first. *Behind the mill* is behind the mill, although that's the inciting event of course.

In stories like this, brutality is common and necessary for moving the plot forward. I do not mean the chopping off of hands or the continuing mentions of *stumps*. I mean how the father says "Help me in my need . . ." I mean the wife who must have looked on. The mother-in-law who butchered a doe for its tongue to pretend she'd killed the girl; who knew to lace the baby tight to the back of the girl so she could walk and walk and walk, as long as she might need.

In stories like this, some people can say "don't touch me" and they'll be heard—some people can say "back up" at close quarters and their particular boundaries are observed—but some people have to include "please" before those requests, soften their tones, because the mask hides their appeasing smiles.

In the story, the girl drew a circle around herself with chalk and the devil couldn't touch her. Tears washing her clean.

In related stories, a girl may wake with no feeling in her hands. If it's because she sleeps on her side, arms and hands curled fetal, there's little to worry about. If the numbness persists—or her hands become useless—there may be something to worry about.

In the story, the girl's hands grew back but she kept her love-made silver hands to prove who she was. She'd need to prove she was the girl bartered to the devil, married to a king, banished, but always pious, always good, never wanting vengeance.

If you have ever been a girl without hands, you may dread being touched—even by your beloved, your loved ones. It comes unbidden sometimes, back of your throat like a second tongue. If there is anything good about this time of enforced distance, it's that sometimes saying "don't touch me" will be heard.

One possible message of the tale: draw yourself a chalk circle to stay safe.

One possible message of the tale: once you start walking, don't ever stop walking.

One possible message of the tale: when someone says "help me in my need," be sure they articulate that "need"—when they say "forgive me of the evil I am going to do to you," look for the shining blade.

Stories like this are *overdetermined*. In this instance, a richness. In other cases, this may be a confusion. There are so many people you cannot trust; there are so many people you can trust.

In related stories, girls subject to brutality after brutality rarely survive intact; chalk circles don't last. Today's girls-without-hands hide in passive voice—are found in second-person point-of-view.

In related stories, people can't hold the line with their voices or their bodies, and are rarely able to survive without wanting vengeance. Hands don't grow back, and the silver hands (love-made), that proof you once withstood whatever the world gave you, aren't something you strap to your back and carry. They're something you lay down and leave.

Personal Mythologies

At the gas station, I hold open the door
but the man behind me—older, white—refuses
the kindness & opens its twin. A younger Black man
walks through the space I've held, stomping his boots.
The old man stares at us : we meet eyes in the wake
of his many signaled disapprovals & maybe
we are saying some version of the same thing
to each other—or maybe not.

This town could be variously described
as a large small town or a very
small city, but either way, it is mostly white
by census & disposition. The kind of white
refracted in terms like blue-collar or working-class
codified by United States v. Bhagat Singh Thind.

There is a man I love, a good friend, and we nearly
lost each other last year. Once the stories of transgressions
moved beyond the monsters, to grey areas, to debates
about category collapse versus category errors,
what I'd taken for long-standing respect & trust
evaporated as quickly as if it had never been.

To make our way back I had to make him listen: to do that,
I had to tell him things I'd never told anyone. I don't know
if he understands what that cost me. The first iterations

of British tanks took two forms: either with machine guns, or
machine guns and 6-pounder Hotchkiss guns.
They were thus gendered female or male, some less able
to defend themselves than others.
Then again, there were warriors who painted female genitals
on their shields as protection against any known enemy.
Things are made at the coercion point:
language, policy, myth.

We're friends again, he & I, but don't work together
anymore. When he offered his unqualified apology, and I
accepted, he gave me a hug—a rare gesture
of physical affection, and kissed
the top of my head—confirming my deepest worry

I cannot escape being a woman. Leaving the gas station

we three are back at the door. The white man holds the door,
and motions only me through.

Poem about the Time You Were Almost a Fairy-Tale Heroine

Mostly sand, and mostly smiles, and mostly you remember it fondly but recently you saw a tweet that said something about *odd things* that happened when you were young that now you know were *fucked up*

He was a photographer, he said. And you were beautiful, he said, and he'd love to take your picture, he said, and he gave you his card.

You don't remember what he looked like.

In fairy tales, people transform, often with kisses: beasts into princes, frogs into princes. Maybe the photographer was a prince or a beast or a frog. But when you said "I'm 15," he turned back into a man, said "I'm sorry," and walked away.

For Jennifer, Who Wants a Job Where She Thinks Up the Names of Racehorses & Lipstick

If not yet budded out, winter-bare, you can see around curves,
corners. The day wine-dark: the road ends in a T,
wide maw becoming county trunk. It is a real road;
a road in dreams, this recurring wool-clot: layers
and layers of color-felt, dross-matt, batting-thick:

The first house on the left was the sometimes-weekend house
of a little girl who needed a breathing mask & heart rate
monitor to sleep. Once it was forgotten, and
the father told the babysitter not to worry. She could
sleep next to the child with her hand
on her chest; if the heart stopped beating, the babysitter
would surely feel it, wake & shake awake the child.
The babysitter may have never recovered; may have decided
then & there, to never have this responsibility
a heart held in her hand; the babysitter
may still have nightmares about children
she's forgotten to tend.

Further on the left a turn leads to a farmhouse
no one farms. Empty silos and barns and broken-down coops

and for a while a boy she loved. For a little while
something lived in the girl & died in the girl.

The next curve curves left and the car drifts to a lake road
where branches branch across all-day shade.
In the brown-shingled house a grandmother & grandfather
died years apart. Every day, the grandmother
who didn't know her own name, her children's, her
granddaughter's, would search rooms & cupboards
looking only for him. Wool is not hair—scale & crimp

differentiate: attaches for easier spinning. She taught the girl
spinning when she remembered her name.
Shadow to the right: periphery, elastic.

At the community center for a baby shower, the woman's
mother nods across the room, where the soon-to-be mother
stands in an oversized man's t-shirt, a sateen ribbon
tied high over her burgeoning. The mother puts
her hand on her daughter's shoulder, juts her chin
in the direction of the soon-to-be, says to her daughter,
"See, she's living with her mistake."

The daughter looks down at her grasping hands. Those hands
will gather the used serving utensils and wash them
in the communal sink. They will collect the paper
plates & napkins, printed with cartoon storks, and crumple

66

into the garbage. Those hands will grip the steering wheel
and drive down the road (real & imagined) to the highway, to
the interstate, and away from this place she used to call home.

When we drive, I always ask "What's the cross street?"
needing to know my bearings.

Marriage Casket

Beneath the steep-gables of my grandparents' cottage,
we had a chest filled with stiff grey blankets & moth balls
to keep out the mice. The box

mine now, plain, not decorated & mostly empty.
The painted panels that decorated early marriage caskets,
though beautifully done, are strange:
the story of Lisabetta da Messina tells of a girl whose beloved
was killed by her brothers. She retrieved his head & kept it
in a vase. It sprouted with the only sweet
her woman's life would have: basil, the tender

green cut into salad & sauce. I hope
the vase sat atop her chest; empty vessels.

Gifts for daughters might be linens & layettes, some
lingerie. Things we might night need later life. Fancy work
tatting to dress some drudgery. My friend tells
me the last time she went through security,

TSA pulled her aside after the full body scan for an invasive
search. Few words between them, but several pairs of hands.
She tried to explain her aberrant body:

what was missing—the amorphous space
visible in black & white. I hope she was
calm as she named the emptiness inside her.
She doesn't fly anymore.

In the stylized geography of horror, there is a location
called The Terrible Place—usually underground,
dark & wet. Both the beginning & end
of something, associated with the womb.
I hope my high-school love knew, when
we broke into my grandparents' cottage in winter,
made an unwise fire—burning first the decorative birch—that
all the things I promised were untrue.
That I was an empty vessel, *something malformed inside.*
Not even an herb could sprout from me,
not one single sprig of green. Maybe
that's why I never had a hope chest,

no box to dress my future wifery. But if I did, I would want
the squarest of corners : panels painted
with *Eros & Anteros.* Winged love, answered love,
neither boxed nor bound.

Ornaments & Armaments

I didn't witness the fight, but I heard
about it: our friends dragging you out,
shards of clear double-pane
from the front window, curved
green stipple from the bottom of bottles.
You started it—bloodied jaw, broken nose.

Fischer's Principle refers to a 1:1 ratio
between females & males, yet the choosy sex
selects for the future breeding success
of their "sexy sons." Over time, a secondary sex
characteristic becomes exaggerated:
some showy ornament. The heritable allele
passes on in sons; daughters inherit the preference.

Another scene you described to me:
you shouldn't have been driving. Your car in the ditch
and your lean frame backlit by the winter light.
Each time I see you now, my eyes
trace the scar down your face.

Scars aren't heritable. I don't know if reckless behavior
is—whether we can map the genes where those traits wait.

Maybe you have them. Me too. I know that road—the way
to the little dam, past the mill pond, between fish camps
and hook-ups for vacation trailers. The county doesn't bother
with the speed limit there, only triangular yellow caution
signs. You were on that road

because I went home with someone
I shouldn't have; it would have been more dangerous
to go home with you. The moon that night rose impossibly
large, some pungent orange just this side of spoiling.

What drew me to you: your angular chin, sharp jawline—
the kind of face studies suggest women prefer
when they're ovulating; the kinds of jobs you worked—
scraping roadkill for a pit in the woods, collecting
euthanized animals from the shelter, taking them
for burning. I wanted to locate some tenderness in you.

Years later, you were a *sneaker male*
in our living room, taking time when someone else
wasn't. Our evolutionary strategies may be subconscious,
but that doesn't mean they don't work. You sat on couches
in living rooms of so many friends, and eventually it paid off.

Running wild, sexual selection can lead to extinction,
like a theory about the Irish Elk growing antlers
so elaborate they tangled in trees & starved.

Natural selection intercedes, stopping a runaway danger.
I never bred. But I brake hard
for eye shine at the shoulder of the road, each
& every glimmer, whether alive & furred, or the twisted metal
of some loss come before, caught in the stiff ditch weed.

For long minutes I've waited as a family of raccoons
froze and darted and froze again
in the glare of headlights some fall evening,
asphalt wet-black with precipitation
caught between rain and ice.

The car's exhaust made a warm fog and still the damn family
of animals wouldn't move. My safer choice asleep
in the passenger seat and he didn't wake either.
Inch forward but no sudden moves—
no one else is coming this time, this particular night.

In Traffic, and then the Seams Unravel

A black Chevy Suburban, seventh generation, either late 70's or early 80's. Rust beyond cosmetic. Rear window panel rolled all the way down into the rear door. In the front sit two boys with baseball caps, a girl between them. All look straight ahead. The wind blows through the open windows, catching stray hair, fluttering sleeves, rustling wrappers and such discarded on the floorboards.

You bristle. Or you don't.

The first warm day of summer, sun-cracked vinyl seats. A ride with your brothers, boy cousins, neighborhood boys. Just three weeks ago on a Saturday it was snowing.

You may remember an offer of a ride, you reach for the back door. "No," one of them says, "sit up front with us." You are too smart to understand, too stupid. Too young. Too loved.

Black vinyl cracks in sunlight, in freeze, reveals the orange-tinted foam fill, weeping its furred insides. The edges of vinyl serrate, cut and prick. The seams unravel, plastic thread like spools of dental floss, spun plastic, too tough to finger wrap and sever. Snag. Bother. Black vinyl seats burn thighs even on the first day of summer baked beyond the pane of glass rolled up.

Or you don't. Bristle.

Brothers or boy cousins or neighborhood boys take you for a ride, catching you on the way home from school. The way older boys' skin felt bracing against your own. The way they smiled crookedly out of the sides of their mouths as they turned off the main road.

The trees, just budding, crowd the narrow one-lane. Up and up before the crest and drop as the asphalt falls away. "Close your eyes," one of them says. You do. Ever obedient. We called them *ticklish hills*, these belly-flop drops, but you had to have enough speed, to pretend you didn't know what was coming—look up or away, best yet: close your eyes. Be surprised by what you know is coming.

[and what if I told you I never wanted a son]

He's been lying there since 1996, known by the moniker
"Green Boots," for the fluorescent Koflach boots he wears.
Snow falls, drifts, covers & uncovers. He has become
a marker, a signpost, harbinger. His mistaken identity

may have led to at least one more dead. Who knows
what his mother thinks. I am not

a mother, but I am a woman, so I think
first of his mother. Another mother, the mother
of the man who died beside him, mistaken for him
and left for dead, insisted her son's body
be brought home after waiting on the mountain
for a year. There are some

estimated two-hundred bodies on Everest:
left in plain sight, tucked into crevices, fallen and fallen.
Climbers step over and around, measure their progress
by these happenstance markers of their fellow questers.
Writing of biography, Bromwich explains
it "define[s] the range
of plausible interpretations of an author."

A group of grandmothers mark themselves Catholic
with a mixture of soot and breast milk
with the sign of the cross
for the coming forced migration.
Perhaps the hand-lettered markings, hand-stabbed

into wrists, forearms, chests

would protect the girls & women from whatever

was coming. The milk

must come from a mother nursing a boy-child.
This was occupied Bosnia, these were Ethnic Croatians.
Some kind of double magic: milk meant for a boy-child
stolen to inoculate the skin stolen by other
boy-children grown to men. Sports psychologists
who research climbers and why they climb
argue against the *thrill theory*, George
Mallory be damned. Many struggle
in their personal relationships and Everest
an escape from all that:
a bruising, boring, endurance-testing escape lasting months.
Waiting-at-base-camp months. Adapting-to-altitude months.
Leave-the-wife-at-home months.
Avoid-family-&-all-its-demands months.

Sometimes, middle of the night, I inhale, making a sound
like ignition. I might combust. After those women
were tattooed, with the milk and whatever grime,

they wrapped their bloodied parts in a rag and didn't wash
for at least a day. If you read in a biography, or a novel
that is thinly fictionalized, some lovely moment
please know *nostalgia,*
particularly for childhood, is likely to be a mask
for unrecognized anger.[1]

---

[1] Carolyn B. Heilbrun, from *Writing a Woman's Life*

Home Remedy : *the witnessing body*[2]

Perhaps a part of a simple Mesopotamian diet, unfurled, loose
leafed. The Egyptians mentioned it,
and if the Greeks ate it, it was simple, dressed
in vinegar. The body unfurls, its own particular
smells, like cabbages, called

brassica, related to various cruciferous vegetables. Brassica
has its uses, like lowering milk supply or weaning.
Likely, it's just the leaves
of certain varieties
are the right shape, chilled
from the refrigerator, with the center stem
cut out, after being washed in the sink
to remove any pesticide residue.

Use the green cabbage. Red will leave tell-tale marks
on skin, and anything
that touches skin. And if you are suppressing milk
for a reason other than weaning

you will see the purple marks and think of bruising,

---

[2] all italics from "Her Body, Himself: Gender in the Slasher Film" Carol J.
Clover

think the body is bringing forth evidence of its own pain.

Years later when your best friend breaks down, apologizing
all the while, saying she's always wished
you had children, that there was a little you,
that you had a daughter too, you will tell her
you are happy with her choice : you will tell her
to shut the fuck up.

Studies that have tried to isolate whatever is in cabbage
have been inconclusive:
1980s Cabbage Patch Kids were a bizarre marketing campaign:
it's only that the leaves curve & cup, around worms & beetles
& ants, things hidden. When the stem is carefully cut out
the nipple stays free. *What makes horror*

"crucial enough to pass along" is, for critics since Freud
what has made ghost stories and fairy tales crucial enough
to pass along:

your breast like any other—your mother's maybe
or the coworker in the cubicle across, the one
you knitted that blanket for, in its own shade of green.
When she told you it was a girl, you laced raspberry-red
around the edge. When she whispered
the name—taken from her grandmother's—you thought
of cabbage. The curve & cup, the hidden things, how to tuck

the name inside & send it back. *We are both*
Red Riding Hood and *the Wolf;*

the force of the experience, the horror, comes from "knowing"
both sides of the story—your co-worker lost
the baby, something you worried, as you worked
the hook of twisted ply in & out the edge of green.
You worried you caused it—that the gift carried its curse
your woman's worry veined in the naming & knowing.

Sound Pedagogies

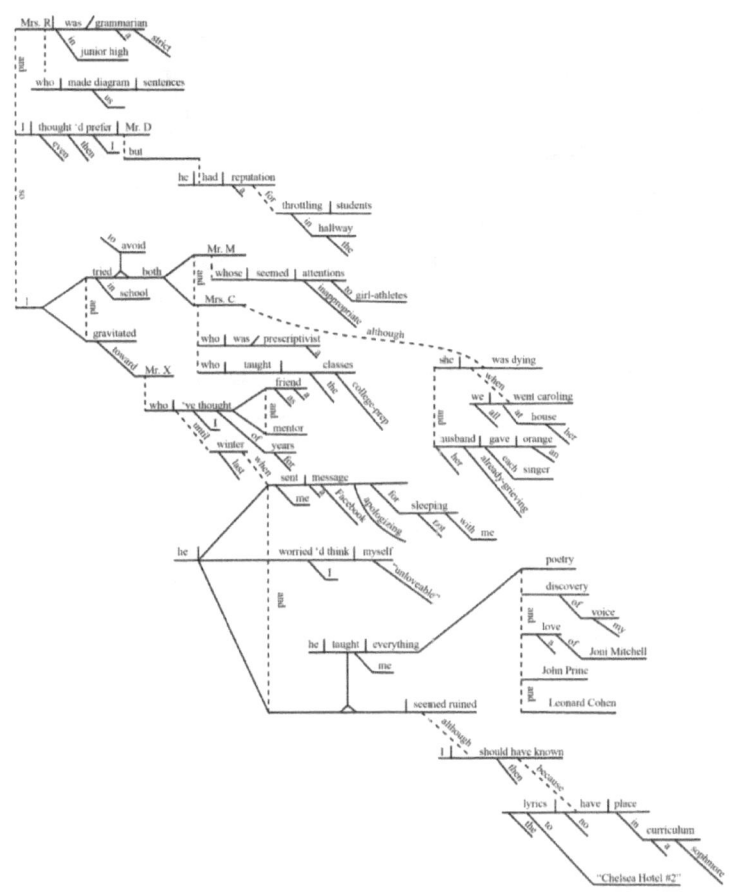

In junior high, Mrs. R was a strict grammarian who made us diagram sentences, and even then I thought I'd prefer Mr. D (but he had a reputation for throttling students in the hallway), so in high school I tried to avoid both Mr. M, whose attentions to girl-athletes seemed inappropriate, and Mrs. C, who was a prescriptivist who taught the college-prep classes (although when she was dying we all went caroling at her house, and her already-grieving husband gave each singer an orange), and gravitated toward Mr. X who I've thought of for years as a friend and mentor—until last winter when he sent me a Facebook message apologizing for not sleeping with me, worried I'd think myself "unloveable," and everything he taught me seemed ruined: poetry, discovery of my voice, and a love of Joni Mitchell, John Prine, and Leonard Cohen, although I should have known then, because the lyrics to "Chelsea Hotel #2" have no place in a sophomore curriculum.

Within the Reed-Kellogg system
a base line contains
the simple sentence and a vertical line
that extends through the base separates
subject from predicate. In teaching
grammar, a proper sentence
must have both, and the predicate
is a verb and its object (at least implied).

Where it becomes difficult—
to parse or diagram—
is whether the object is direct
or indirect. Should the line
be straight or a backslash, signaling
the earlier subject? Other modifiers
hang below the base line
placed according to what
they alter. What seems
simple takes on layers,
hangers-on, additional weight.

They are everywhere: Mr. X — Dr. Why — *just call me Zeee*

Cf: the choice of texts.

Sunlight fights its way through the window's grime. Whatever you've done to survive is the least dirty thing in the room.

The Amusements

Performance Art for Middle-Aged Women

She swallows bees, one only, one
at a time. Closes her mouth and lets it bump & travel
the soft places inside her—mouth to belly and back again.

Esophageal flesh, all pink & wet & glisten.

Sometimes the bee stings, depositing
its bitter toxin, strobing heartbeat & bloodrunning; sometimes
the bee does its disoriented dance
and dies, small body intact, still owning
its barbed stinger, only harmed and not harming.

Open the soft space of your body and invite
pain in. Imagine the crazed flight, body
full of danger pheromones, a cloud of confused hive
surrounds you, and not one of the bee's she-army comrades
able to find the source.

Bess Knows from Being Buried Alive

Because she was a showgirl (because first she considered his
brother)

Because she wore a size one shoe, never bled, threw her hat back
when her anger hadn't dissipated, may have slipped him a key in a
glass of water or a kiss (because

she would always be his second love)   there's something
                                                     about boys &
                                                     their mums, men
                                                     & their
                                                     mothers—at least
                                                     they knew who
                                                     made heaven &
                                                     earth, who
                                                     turned down the
                                                     covers & stoked
                                                     the coal

Because together they kept a menagerie of pets, of dolls, of secrets,
                                        of tricks

(because she held séances for ten years after his death, then gave
up, declaring that
long enough
to wait for any man)

Because she knew he knew something about confinement: the
milk can, the
straitjacket, the
crate lowered into water, body manacled inside.

(because you will walk the darkness of the house in the absence of
others and find
any old thing,
and think: *this will hold—this will fit.*)

Because there will be times you will be both more & less than
your body
when you will
wonder what a
shoulder socket
can do, carefully
trained; when
you wonder what
lungs can do,
beyond full
capacity; what
playbills

proclaim; when
even your spouse
will not know
what you are
capable of

Middle America

Dita Von Teese once said her favorite shoes
weren't for walking—literally—they were made
to crawl in. If you listen closely, all over the homes
of certain childhoods in middle America, you can hear
the plastic on the couch crinkle. I've never understood
what's meant by *the good china*; I put the gilt-rimmed plates
in the microwave to see them spark. My grandmother's Spode
down to four plates, and when my mother visits
she tells me to pack it away, for safe keeping, for later.

The clear wrap still ringing her buff-colored lamp shades
may be for protection, or simply
a sign of inattention, but visiting for the weekend
I unwind in the dark & discard. Last week,
I dusted off my one pair of heels to wear to a fundraiser
and told everyone—not wanting them to mistake me
for the kind of woman who wears heels regularly.

Scholars disagree as to whether it was ever possible
to move elegantly in chopines, those platformed
noblewoman's shoes. Two servants needed
to affix them to the feet; two others
to assist with walking; but maybe with practice

one could dance. Jeweled or embroidered to match a gown
that hung down well over their tops, obscuring the extra work.
Shakespeare quipped about *altitude*; Venetian sumptuary laws
regulated their height. If I'm going to crawl,

my bare feet will make sparks.
Whatever's unwound in the dark won't be couch-crinkle quiet.

Kith & Kin

The first time I remember thinking about lactation
a finger dragged its way from the small of my back up
between shoulder blades. Pseudo-friend, pseudo-family
we called Uncle said he *couldn't wait to taste it.*

Revulsion, a hot blush, kissing cousin to shame, close enough
to the other things bodies do, at least once, in the dark
if they're led upstairs by the hand.

indelible in the hippocampus

It was either Town X or Town Y, both just shy of an hour from home. It was either "Rump Shaker" or "O.P.P." It was one of those single cassette tapes—we bought those then—stuck in the car's stereo, and it played over and over and over.   I was in the passenger seat looking out the rolled-up window
        then I was huddled against the black vinyl door handle
        then I was grateful for the stick shift he got caught on
        then I was doing whatever I was able to do with my hands
/ the nails I'd grown / the small fists I made / what voice I had
        then I took to the floor, knees up & curled, fitting myself tight into the wheel well, my back hot & heating from the down vent

it hadn't yet snowed

various interpretations of "O.P.P." make this more or less relevant; all I remember of "Rump Shaker" is the video

this boy was very white, in his Midwestern muscle car

this boy said, *Jesus*—, he said it was *too much work*

I've become one of those single cassette tapes lately, playing on repeat: at cigarette breaks, around the bonfire, every time I hear doubt

I remember central details too, but the peripheral have disappeared: Town X or Town Y, his full name. But I know we were in the parking lot of a grocery store after hours, and he parked behind a dumpster that blocked the view of anyone driving by; I remember *after,* standing in his perfectly-normal kitchen, waiting for my ride home

Sawing Through a Woman

The trick requires separate compartments : different women :
                    she is unduly flexible : extremely patient

Above the waist, she must be neuter: a minimizing bra
or binder; button-down shirt with no gaping—no suggestion
of burgeoning or tumescence; a jacket
with a least two buttons, preferably three (the key
is containment); any fitting, any feminine touch
(a peplum or bit of lace) must
be balanced by conservative neutrals:
grey, navy, black.

Below the waist, she must be all femme: a fitted skirt
hits above the knee. Her legs exposed, shapely
and hairless. The legs must
hint at the way she clefts & clefts, how she will
cleave & cleave.

In some variations, there is more than one blade, serrated
or dull. For instance, perhaps
the shoes—always high-heeled, pointy-toed—are also
severed.

For instance, in some iterations, members of the audience
are invited to wrap
ropes around her arms, legs or neck, and hold tight.
The "Wakeling Variation" utilizes a collar
around her neck, weighted with heavy chain.

For a woman to maintain her bodily integrity
has always been a parlor trick. In boardrooms, conferences,
statehouses, a smattering
of polite applause for her, thunderous
for the man who points & flourishes, who wields
the tool, who holds out his hand to gingerly
assist her back to her feet.

At the Ten-In-One, alongside the Born Freaks are

Working Acts, Strongmen & women with particular talents.
Barkers hint what's behind the curtain. Behind the curtain,

a man is fingerless, digits lost to blast or machine—the magic
what he learns to do with his stumps. Beside him his woman,

attests what he's learned to do with his stumps (not suitable
for women or children, this kootchie show). Strongman's huge;

he's here after being worked like a beast anyway.
No insurance, no-notice rotating shifts, poor safety records

laughed out of the boss's office when he says he wants a job
where he can spend time with his wife, his little girl (as a baby

he could hold her upright in the palm of his hand).
If you're blue-collar, this is what work is:

the beam in the truck springs loose, and at the hospital,
they drug test you before they treat you. When the beam

in the truck springs loose, they'll blame the dockworker
from the Texas-Mexico border in the report.

Put you on light duty, no driving, but make you drive
to work each day to check in. And when your father is dying

you cannot take off, because you didn't request time
two weeks ahead through the manager, the foreman.

Death isn't orderly like lines through the Side Show,
the careful tease of the Barker's script. You've seen

human skeletons, the Fat Lady, the Tattooed Lady,
too much skin & not enough. Jars hold pickled punks,

some strange animals. One sad man reminds you
of your cousin, prescription-addled.

Here comes the Blowoff Act, and they'll ask
for more—they always ask for more.

The Girl Who Wanted

The culvert preserves the stream, the path, the traffic
of people crossing here, where tiny lupine
attract a certain species of butterfly, where
early Cambrian sand can't be farmed,
not well. As kids, we called it

sugar sand. As kids, we Adams soured on power:
the water smells like water smells.
Metallic tang, mud & leaf mold, cold
even high summer. Sneaking away under bridges

had a smell, in the Land of Synesthesia, long-ago afternoons
when parents left you unaccounted for, and older brothers
& their friends lured & tackle-boxed, knew
where fish hid, where mud turtles

waited to be caught. The shock of it, the first
time—all raised flesh, like a welt
a bruise of cooled blue, and your feet sunk
into the particulate marl ankle-deep
unable to move. Water rushes

the carved depth just below the metal & concrete,
whatever you'd sought out and crossed. The water
brown like beer, when beer was something
you hadn't tasted and still wanted.

At Luna Park, the Author is Dead

Because the streets were going to be lit, lines
stretched into homes, illuminating corners & comers,
company men debated how to do this well & efficiently.
The DC folks paid children to collect stray dogs
and in public exhibitions shocked them
first with varying levels of DC current, then AC, until
still. Edison joked the quickest way to kill a man

was to hire him out as a lineman. But New York
wanted to kill men quicker than hanging
and every new technology advantages some, dis
advantages others. The word for this new method of death
was also a debate: Westinghouse'd, Browned, or some variant.
Perhaps names matter; perhaps

something other entirely. The elephant named Topsy
is often mistakenly inserted into the story here, a casualty
of the War of the Currents. This story survives, because
a short film survives: fed cyanide-laced carrots, clad
in copper sandals & electrocuted, then strangled
with ropes tied to a steam-powered winch.

Imagine the 28-year-old circus animal
who'd killed a spectator after
he burned her trunk with a cigar and several times
turned on her captors—the drunken handler,
the publicity-hungry owners. Imagine the final crowd
gathered to cheer on this ultimate spectacle.

Or don't—watch the grainy 74-second film, grim
nickelodeon. Watch her stiffen
in the 6,600 volts—see smoke rise
from her feet. Topsy falls, all flesh & pain. Nb:
there's a gap of nearly two hours,
when she refused to cross the lagoon
to the killing field.

I think of how our friendship ended : Wonder who
flipped the switch.

Types of Closure

We know each other's secrets, each other's pain—
the story that undergirds the stories we would tell.
Even (maybe) the ones we wouldn't tell.
Writers are warned about adverbs: to not dress
up our verbs. Extra syllables weaken, so goes
traditional wisdom. Let verbs muscle the sentence,
no need to qualify or enhance. We once laid

in a late afternoon bedroom
while out the window
indistinct blossoms. You saw best
up close and my eyes
knew things in the distance. This middle range
both our blind spots: their petaled shapes
caught somewhere between
curves, and edged
angles—but we each swore
we knew what we saw, that we could
identify them & write down
their names.

Carry with you a well-designed weapon at all times.
You'll need it for family most of all.

Everyone I know has taken up TIG welding—for practical
reasons, for pleasure. So many metals
can be linked together, given enough time,
a clean workspace and little wind. We like to practice
a skill, again & again, our hands gloved
in leather, as close as possibly safe
to the arcing blue-white light.

Make things that may or may not have a purpose;
join heavy things broken apart.

Vantage Points

We arrive, handfuls of bees and sweat, to wide
front porches and grandparents waiting, cousins
somewhere nearby, unable to sit still, scattered
in the woods or upstairs rooms.
We arrive, road-weary

and slog the air up the stairs to held-open arms
after some interminable travel packed into cars
long hours. The best vantage point the *way back*

a third row seat that faced the retreating road, so
whoever sat there could see where they've been
but never where they were going. That old Volvo

ended up my older brother's teenage ride and once
it lost its doors, a shelter for our family dog before some
local business took it off our hands for the county fair
demolition derby, and eventually some wrecking yard's
crusher ate it. Maybe the left-over bits recycled
into new cars: floor mats or brake pedals
for new sedans and new families

so it's all our vantage point now: no skin to touch or
sweat to exchange, so instead we watch the receding asphalt

ticker ticker ticker of intermittent center line

to parse together what was—middle of some joke
I recount the silvered pad I slept on to curtail bed-wetting;
how what was supposed to buzz shorted
and began to zap—how those mini-shocks worked,
retraining me. My friend—a mother—asks the obvious:
why did you start wetting the bed?

And I don't remember exactly, but know / ticker ticker
ticker / something happened / center line

Next time my mother & I sit across the span of her porch, I ask:
about the shock mat / my regression / about that time

After my emergency appendectomy, two years old,
I started wetting the bed again—a brother
soon-to-be-born, and my mother apologizes

(she says the pad was only supposed to buzz,
not shock, but) she was so tired, couldn't handle
the idea of two of us in diapers—

they tried everything: an old fainting couch moved
into my room, thinking this lower furniture might help
me get up easier (and I remember it, purple velour, bolster
pillow), her overwhelmed. I knew it was something / ticker

ticker ticker / center line / some event: she mentions

that surgery, my brother's birth, the dog attack that scars
my face. Some whitened memory of the emergency room,
how the doctor wouldn't let me have a mirror,
no matter how many times I asked—
so my recollection is sense memory: fingertips
magnify what's there, the sutures and ties and
puckers of skin reattached to skin. One theory
is that female dogs are more aggressive during heat cycles;
another that my appearance triggered some response
in her—she'd bit another similar-looking girl in the past.

I say I don't remember much of my childhood
before eight or nine, but there are these moments

shock mat / anesthesia / fingertips

finding the contours of a wound. The way-back seat
allows us to only look back. Windshields pop
and metal squeals but someday we'll approach

each other closer and closer, not measuring distance
and stopping before we touch. As my mother says,
there was so much going on.

Highwire

Inside a tension-tent, rows of chairs
wait for the day's event. The open center lofts upward.

Funambulists have been antidote against melancholy
since the 5th century French ban was lifted. But each
stunt demanded greater: farther & farther distances, props,
weighted down by washing machines or wearing
peach baskets spanning Niagara Falls. Like that friend
on Friday nights, who makes his body a party—
moving ball joints in their shallow sockets, popping
them out to watch others' faces crumple
in phantom pain. If he suffers, he doesn't show it, but
the name for what he has is *hypermobility syndrome*;
there's no such thing as double-jointed.

Start on a slack line strung low; research
suggests information about the body's movements
in response to the line's movements
coalesce in the inner ear. The study
identifies an optimal sag of three feet

to manage the feedback loop of unsteady surface,
tensed body & constant corrections.

The body's center mass must stay above the base of support.

Watch the shoulders: know the slump
that means a coming falter or flail. Under the tented
skin space magnifies; like those
who can extend their joints
beyond normal range or those who gather an audience
for greater and greater feats. We are each other's net
until we aren't.

Aftermath

My father told me to
turn the lights on when the sky
got soft & greenish grey—after the F-scale winds,
when people might be picking their way
through the wreckage of what was home,
and ours untouched

we had a roof, food, electricity.

Come spring, we'd clean the mice
out of the bucket of used motor oil
in the garage, silken lumps fished out of a skein
of treacle. Used motor oil has many uses beyond
a death-trap for unlikely families in an unlikely place.

We are talking about fathers because both your father
and stepfather had told you *You can't trust anyone
who bleeds five days & doesn't die—*

When there's a storm, I still think we should
get the chainsaw and walk around to the neighbors,
cutting brush, clearing what needs clearing, checking
in. I recognized that lumpen death

smothered in the grey-green of dirty oil
because earlier that year I'd found a nest
in the cap on the propane tank:
pink & hairless, I put them back
before anyone else saw. Viscous-slick,
they'd been tempered to the ultimate vulnerability.

I want to tell you

how down the hill, by the creek, there were these plants
we called Touch-Me-Nots,—some kind of jewelweed
with orange flowers and sweet nectar,
and we'd rub it on broken or itchy skin, but
mostly we liked to poke the cylindrical pods,
watch them split & furl back onto themselves.
In the moted light, we could watch the trajectory
of the seeds. You are surprised
I've never heard that saying, but what I learned

is how to manage lumpen death, a chainsaw, and
to touch everything that claims to not want touch.

ACKNOWLEDGEMENTS

Thank you to the following journals, art spaces, and web platforms where these poems previously appeared: *Entropy Magazine, Figure 1, Roar, Menacing Hedge, Spark Wheel Press, SWIMM Miami, Coffin Bell, Pleiades, the museum of americana, Painted Bride Quarterly, Memoir Mixtapes, Occulum,* the Chazen Art Museum website with their Bridge Poetry Series, former Wisconsin Poet Laureate Margaret Rozga's column in the *Bay View Compass,* and the *Coffin Bell 2020, Local News: Poetry about Small Towns,* and *New Writing from the Midwest 2019* anthologies.

Many thanks to artist Mollie Oblinger who was integral to the forms of "Sound Pedagogies" and "January in Wisconsin"—I can arrange language, but using technology to create the visual on the page is beyond me. You are my refuge.

My Porketta, Jennifer Escher, who encourages me, listens, and has no conversational boundaries (thank gawd for that!). Thank you also to Jennifer D. Sims, insightful reader and careful editor, who has read these poems and this manuscript seven ways from Sunday. Thank you to B.J. Best for reading the manuscript in process and offering a poet's suggestions about shape. And to Bruce Dethlefsen and Cathryn Cofell, poet friends, board game players, and sometimes dancing partners—because we all need a week here and there away from our normal lives.

ABOUT THE AUTHOR

C. Kubasta writes poetry, fiction, and hybrid forms. Her last book was the short-story collection *Abjectification* (Apprentice House). A former professor of writing, literature, and cultural studies, she is now the executive director of Shake Rag Alley Center for the Arts in Mineral Point Wisconsin, which offers arts & crafts workshops for adults and youth. She is passionate about language, rural imagery, and the stories we try not to tell. She's working on herself. Find her at ckubasta.com and follow her @CKubastathePoet

ABOUT THE PRESS

Unsolicited Press is based out of Portland, Oregon and focuses on the works of the unsung and underrepresented. As a womxn-owned, all-volunteer small publisher that doesn't worry about profits as much as championing exceptional literature, we have the privilege of partnering with authors skirting the fringes of the lit world. We've worked with emerging and award-winning authors such as Amy Shimshon-Santo, Brook Bhagat, Elisa Carlsen, Tara Stillions Whitehead, and Anne Leigh Parrish.

Learn more at unsolicitedpress.com. Find us on Instagram, X, Facebook, Pinterest, Bsky, Threads, YouTube, and LinkedIn. Unsolicited Press also writes a snarky newsletter on Substack.

www.ingramcontent.com/pod-product-compliance
Lightning Source LLC
Chambersburg PA
CBHW031428120626
46545CB00006B/2313